GALE
CENGAGE Learning

Novels for Students, Volume 3 Copyright Notice

Gale Research
835 Penobscot Building
645 Griswold St.
Detroit, MI 48226-4094

This book is printed on acid-free paper that meets the minimum requirements of American National Standard for Information Sciences—Permanence Paper for Printed Library Materials, ANSI Z39.48-1984.

ISBN 0-7876-2113-7
ISSN 1094-3552

Printed in the United States of America.
10 9 8 7 6 5 4

Their Eyes Were Watching God

Zora Neale Hurston

1937

Introduction

When *Their Eyes Were Watching God* first appeared in 1937, it was well-received by white critics as an intimate portrait of southern blacks, but African-American reviewers rejected the novel as pandering to white audiences and perpetuating stereotypes of blacks as happy-go-lucky and ignorant. Unfortunately, the novel and its author, Zora Neale Hurston, were quickly forgotten. But within the last twenty years it has received renewed attention from scholars who praise its unique contribution to African-American literature, and it has become one of the newest and most original works to consistently appear in college courses across the country and to be included in updated versions of the American literary canon. The book has been admired by African-Americanists for its celebration of black culture and dialect and by feminists for its depiction of a woman's progress towards selfawareness and fulfillment. But the novel continues to receive criticism for what some see as its lack of engagement with racial prejudice and its ambivalent treatment of relations between the sexes. No one disputes, though, its impressive use of metaphor, dialect, and folklore of southern rural blacks, which Hurston studied as an anthropologist, to reflect the rich cultural heritage of African Americans.

Author Biography

Zora Neale Hurston's colorful life was a strange mixture of acclaim and censure, success and poverty, pride and shame. But her varied life, insatiable curiosity, and profound wit made her one of the most fascinating writers America has known. Even her date of birth remains a mystery. She claimed in her autobiography to have been born on 7 January 1903, but family members swore she was born anywhere from 1891 to 1902. Nevertheless, it is known that she was born in Eatonville, Florida, which was to become the setting for most of her fiction and was the first all-black incorporated town in the nation. Growing up there, where her father was mayor, Hurston was largely sheltered from the racial prejudice African Americans experienced elsewhere in America.

At the age of fourteen, Hurston struck out on her own, working as a maid for white families, and was sent to Morgan Academy in Baltimore by one of her employers. Her educational opportunities continued to grow. She studied at Barnard College, where she worked under the eminent anthropologist Franz Boas. She also attended Howard University, and Columbia University, where she began work towards a Ph.D. in anthropology.

Hurston published her first story in 1921 and quickly gained recognition among the writers of the newly formed Harlem Renaissance, an outpouring of artistic innovation in the African-American community of Harlem. She moved there in 1925 with little money but much ambition, and became well-known as the most colorful member of the artistic and literary circles of the city. She also gained the attention of Mrs. Rufus Osgood Mason, a wealthy white patron who agreed to fund Hurston's trips to Florida where she gathered folklore. Although she married Herbert Sheen during this period, they lived together only eight months before her career came between them. While they split amicably, a later marriage to Albert Price III, which lasted from 1939 to 1943, ended bitterly.

Hurston's career as a novelist picked up in the 1930s. Her first novel, *Jonah's Gourd Vine*, appeared in 1934 and became a Book-of-the-Month Club selection. The following year, she published *Mules and Men*, a collection of folktales that mixed anthropology and fiction. This book gained her widespread recognition and helped her win a Guggenheim fellowship to study folklore in the West Indies. Before leaving for Haiti, she fell in love with a younger man. When he demanded that she give up her career, she ended the affair, but wrote the novel *Their Eyes Were Watching God* in seven weeks, translating their romance into the relationship between Janie and Tea Cake. The novel appeared in 1937 to some recognition and controversy, but it quickly receded from the limelight and was not a commercial success.

Although she published two more novels, another book of folklore, and dozens of stories,

Hurston's literary reputation dwindled throughout the 1940s and '50s. In 1948 she was charged with committing an immoral act with a ten-year-old boy and was later absolved of the crime, but the damage to her public reputation had been done. Hurston felt that she was forever outcast from the African-American literary community of Harlem, so she spent the rest of her life in Florida, where she worked various jobs and tried to keep her head above water financially. When she suffered a stroke in 1959, she was committed to a welfare home where she died penniless and alone in 1960. She was buried in an unmarked grave in the segregated cemetery of Fort Pierce. The location remained unknown until 1973, when it was located by author Alice Walker.

Plot Summary

Chapter 1

Zora Neale Hurston's *Their Eyes Were Watching God* opens with a lyrical passage in which Janie Starks returns to her previous home, Eatonville. The other townspeople observe her in judgment and speculate about what has brought her back. Through their dialogue, the characters of Pheoby, Janie's best friend, and Tea Cake, the young man she left with, are introduced. Eventually, Pheoby visits Janie, who tells her that Tea Cake is "gone." The rest of the novel will consist of the story Janie tells Pheoby about what has happened to her.

Chapters 2 through 4

Janie summarizes her childhood, when she lived with her maternal grandmother, Nanny, who also cared for several white children. At one point, a photographer takes a picture of all of the children. While examining the photograph, Janie realizes that she is black; until then she had thought she was like all of the white children. One spring afternoon years later, Janie is daydreaming under a pear tree when Johnny Taylor appears and kisses her. Nanny observes this and decides that Janie ought to get married soon. She has decided on Brother Logan Killicks as Janie's future husband; he is apparently a responsible man, but Janie does not find him attractive and cannot imagine loving him. But Janie and Logan are married, and shortly thereafter Nanny dies.

Sometime later, Logan decides that Janie should perform more manual labor and leaves to buy a mule so that Janie can help him with the plowing. While he is gone, another man appears, a stranger to the area who identifies himself as Joe Starks. He is on his way to a town populated entirely by black people, where he has large ambitions for himself. Although Joe invites Janie to accompany him, she hesitates because she imagines how her grandmother would disapprove. When Janie threatens to leave Logan, he scorns her background. The next morning she meets Joe Starks, and they travel to Green Cove Springs where they are married.

Chapters 5 through 9

Joe and Janie arrive in Eatonville, where Joe immediately asks to speak to the mayor and is informed that the town does not have one. Impressing the others, Joe pays cash for two hundred acres of land and begins advertising for additional people to move to Eatonville. After opening a store, Joe is soon appointed Mayor, but discord comes when he prevents Janie from making a speech some of the men have requested. Joe and Janie begin to grow apart emotionally.

Many of the men enjoy sitting on the store's

porch and telling exaggerated stories. Although Janie longs to join in, Joe believes such activities and company are too low-class for her. Another man, Matt Bonner, owns a mule that he is working nearly to death. When Janie expresses dismay over the abuse of this mule, Joe forces Matt to sell the mule for five dollars. After the mule dies, Joe again forbids Janie to participate in the mock funeral with the rest of the town.

The tension between Joe and Janie continues to intensify, until one day Joe slaps her because his supper has been poorly cooked. Janie's image of Joe is destroyed at this moment, and although she appears to continue to be obedient, she begins separating her inner and outer lives. Then one day when Janie fails to cut a plug of tobacco properly, Joe humiliates her in front of the others, commenting on aspects of her body. This time Janie replies, ridiculing Joe for his own lack of masculinity in front of the other men. Joe is so angry that he can respond only by hitting her.

Joe subsequently becomes ill and believes Janie has cast a spell on him. Janie sends for a doctor, who reveals that Joe's condition is fatal. Although Janie attempts to have a final conversation with him, Joe refuses to listen and dies fighting death. His funeral is large and formal.

Chapters 10 through 13

After several months, another stranger appears. His name is Vergible Woods, but his nickname is

Tea Cake. He teaches Janie to play checkers, and for the first time she feels that someone is truly treating her as an individual. They do many unconventional activities together, such as fishing at midnight, and Janie begins to fall in love with him. She hesitates to trust him, though, because she is several years older than he is and because, as Joe's heir, she is a comparatively wealthy woman. Janie decides to sell the store so that she can begin a new life with Tea Cake. He sends for her from Jacksonville, and she leaves on an early morning train. They get married immediately.

Janie has hidden two hundred dollars in a purse inside her clothes, but when she wakes up the next morning, Tea Cake is gone and so is the money. After another day, he returns with only twelve dollars; he had thrown a party but promises to win the money back gambling. When he does, Janie decides to trust him and tells him about additional money she has saved. Tea Cake suggests that they go down to the Everglades to work.

Chapters 14 through 17

Tea Cake teaches Janie to shoot, and she becomes quite skilled. Working in the Everglades is fun for both of them; they throw parties, and Janie participates in the playful atmosphere. Janie becomes jealous of another woman who is flirting with Tea Cake, but he assures Janie that she has nothing to worry about. They decide to stay in the Everglades during the off season. Another woman,

Mrs. Turner, cultivates a friendship with Janie, hoping that she will leave Tea Cake and marry Mrs. Turner's brother. Mrs. Turner feels disdainful of other black people, especially if their complexion is particularly dark. At this point, Tea Cake becomes jealous and beats Janie in order to demonstrate to the Turners that he is boss in his household.

Chapters 18 through 20

A hurricane threatens the Everglades, and many of the residents leave, but Janie and Tea Cake decide to ride the storm out. When the storm becomes fierce, they sit in their cabin, appearing "to be staring at the dark, but their eyes were watching God." When the hurricane threatens to flood their house, they leave, attempting to walk toward Palm Beach. When Janie is nearly attacked by a dog, Tea Cake rescues her, but he is bitten. The wound appears superficial and begins to heal.

> The dog stood up and growled like a lion, stiff-standing hackles, stiff muscles, teeth uncovered as he lashed up his fury for the charge. Tea Cake split the water like an otter, opening his knife as he dived. The dog raced down the back-bone of the cow to the attack and Janie screamed and slipped far back on the tail of the cow, just out of reach of the dog's angry jaws. He wanted to plunge in after her but dreaded the water,

> somehow. Tea Cake rose out of the water at the cow's rump and seized the dog by the neck. But he was a powerful dog and Tea Cake was overtired. So he didn't kill the dog with one stroke as he had intended. But the dog couldn't free himself either. They fought and somehow he managed to bite Tea Cake high up on his cheek-bone once. Then Tea Cake finished him and sent him to the bottom to stay there. The cow relieved of a great weight was landing on the fill with Janie before Tea Cake stroked in and crawled weakly upon the fill again.

After the hurricane, black men are forced to act as grave diggers, but they must be careful to separate the white corpses from the black ones, because the white bodies will be placed in coffins while the black ones will be buried in a mass grave. After one day, Tea Cake decides they should return to the Everglades.

Three weeks later, Tea Cake falls ill. He has a headache and is unable to eat or drink. The doctor reveals that he has rabies and will likely die. He is concerned that Tea Cake will attack Janie and perhaps bite her also. Janie realizes that Tea Cake is becoming insane as his illness progresses. He eventually tries to shoot Janie, who shoots and kills him.

Janie must be tried for murder, but she is

acquitted; the jury finds that she acted in self-defense. Janie provides an elaborate funeral for Tea Cake in Palm Beach. The novel concludes with a return to the conversation between Janie and Pheoby after Janie has returned to the house she lived in with Joe.

Characters

Janie Crawford

The heroine of the novel, Janie, is the first black woman character in African-American fiction to embark on a journey of self-discovery and achieve independence and self-understanding. But she does not do so until she is nearly forty years old. Many obstacles stand in her way, the first of which is her grandmother, who encourages her to marry Logan Killicks for material security. But Janie discovers that "marriage did not make love," and she decides to leave him. When Joe Starks enters her life, she believes she has found her ticket to the "horizon," so she marries him. But when they arrive in Eatonville, she discovers that she is going to be nothing but an ornament of his power and success. Stifled by Jody and cut off from the rest of the community by her status as the mayor's wife, she learns to hide her real self and wear a mask for Jody and the town that conforms to their expectations for her. But in the process she loses sight of the real self she has buried. The narrator tells us, "She had an inside and an outside now and suddenly she knew not how to mix them." After twenty years of marriage, an enmity has grown between Janie and her husband that results in her finally speaking up for herself. She tells him, in essence, that he is no longer a real man, and her outburst robs him of the will to live. As he lays on his deathbed, she sums up for him what their marriage has been like for her: "Mah own mind had tuh be squeezed and crowded out tuh make room for yours in me."

Having lost herself once, she vows not to do so again, and so she enjoys her freedom after his death. But when Tea Cake walks into her life, she finds a man who complements her search for self-awareness rather than squelches it. Under the influence of his all-encompassing love, "her soul crawled out from its hiding place." With Tea Cake, she finds a spiritual sense of love that had been absent in her first two marriages. "Ah wuz fumblin' round and God opened the door," she tells him. But many critics have questioned Hurston's decision to make Janie discover her true self in the context of a relationship with a man. What has seemed like a feminist search for identity is undermined by Janie's apparent dependence on Tea Cake, some say. But Janie does eventually gain true independence when she is forced to kill Tea Cake, who has gone mad from being bitten by a rabid dog and has come after her with a gun. This final act, although it devastates Janie, also allows her to return home to Eatonville a fully self-sufficient woman who is finally at peace with herself. "Ah done been tuh de horizon and back and now Ah kin set heah in mah house and live by comparisons," she tells her friend Pheoby. Her journey of self-discovery is complete.

Hezekiah

After Jody's death, Hezekiah replaces him as

the store's manager. Janie notices that Hezekiah also begins to take on many of Jody's characteristics.

Jody

See Joe Starks

Janie Killicks

See Janie Crawford

Logan Killicks

Janie's first husband. Her grandmother has encouraged her to marry him because he can give her a house and sixty acres of farmland, hence security. His ugly appearance and body odor prevent Janie from falling in love with him. When he tells her he is going to buy a mule for her to plow with, Janie decides that life with Logan is not what she bargained for. She leaves him when the more dashing Joe Starks comes along.

Motor Boat

A gambling friend of Tea Cake down on the muck. When the hurricane hits, Motor Boat flees with Janie and Tea Cake.

Nanny

Janie's grandmother, who raises her in the absence of her mother. A former slave who was raped by her master, Nanny teaches Janie that the "nigger woman is de mule uh de world." In her hopes that Janie will have a better life, she encourages her to marry Logan Killicks, a man who will offer her "protection." But not long after Janie marries him, Nanny dies. Later in life, after Jody has died, Janie reassesses the advice Nanny had given her. "Nanny had taken the biggest thing God ever made, the horizon … and pinched it in to such a little bit of a thing that she could tie it about her granddaughter's neck tight enough to choke her." Janie decides that she hates Nanny for teaching her to bury her own desires for the sake of security.

Nunkie

Young woman on the muck who attempts to lead Tea Cake away from Janie.

Sop-de-Bottom

A friend of Tea Cake on the muck. He applauds Tea Cake's beating of Janie and attempts to speak up at Janie's trial after she has killed Tea Cake. He wants to accuse Janie of murder but is silenced by a white lawyer.

Janie Starks

See Janie Crawford

Media Adaptations

- *Their Eyes Were Watching God* has been recorded on cassette in an abridged version by Caedmon. This recording, which came out in 1991, was performed by Ruby Dee.
- In 1994, Recorded Books produced an unabridged recording of the novel on sound cassette, read by Michele-Denise Woods.
- The movie rights to the novel are owned by Quincy Jones and Oprah Winfrey, although as of 1997 no film had yet been made.

Joe Starks

Jody rescues Janie from her first marriage,

whisking her off to Eatonville, Florida, an all-black town where he intends to "be a big voice," something he has been denied in other towns where whites are in control. Although Janie is reluctant to go, Jody "spoke for far horizon," offering Janie a chance for adventure. But shortly after they arrive in Eatonville, Janie finds out that her life with Jody will be anything but exciting. When he becomes mayor and the most respectable citizen in town, she becomes a "pretty doll-baby," as he calls her, a token of his stature in the town. Jody defines himself by his position and possessions, the most valuable of which is Janie. So Jody stifles Janie's development as he silences her and keeps her from participating in the town's talk on the porch of their store. Jody's world becomes a kind of prison for Janie, who is isolated on a pedestal of bourgeois ideals. As Jody grows older and takes his fears of aging out on Janie, she realizes that her "image" of him has "tumbled down and shattered." When he ridicules her aging body in front of others at the store, something breaks in Janie, and she tells him, "When you pull down yo' britches, you look lak de change uh life." By belittling his manhood in front of the town, Janie figuratively kills him, as he begins a slow deterioration and dies of kidney failure. Janie attempts to come to terms with Jody on his death bed, and she tells him, "All dis bowin' down, all dis obedience under yo' voice—dat ain't whut Ah rushed off down de road tuh find out about you." But she comes to the conclusion that the only kind of change he was able to create in her life was an outward change in material conditions. Nothing has changed inside of him, and she has not been able to grow at all. When he dies, the only legacy he leaves Janie is his money. At the end of the book, it is the memories of Tea Cake that inhabit the house, not those of Jody.

Johnny Taylor

The boy who kisses Janie over the fence. This event signals Janie's sexual awakening and instigates Nanny's concerns that Janie will allow an unworthy man to lure her away.

Mr. Turner

Restaurant owner on the muck who has no control over his wife.

Mrs. Turner

A light-skinned mulatto woman who befriends Janie on the muck. Her prejudices against those who are blacker than herself reveal the racism within the black community. Her restaurant, which she owns with her husband, is destroyed by Tea

Cake and his friends, who resent her racist attitudes towards them.

Mrs. Annie Tyler

A woman from Eatonville who ran off with a younger man who was after her money. Her shameful return to the town after he has left her is a warning to Janie, who fears that Tea Cake will do the same to her.

Pheoby Watson

Janie's "bosom friend" who is her link to the Eatonville community. Pheoby's role in the book is an important one, as she is the audience for Janie's life story, which is the novel. After hearing the whole story, Pheoby tells her, "Ah done growed ten feet higher from jus' listenin' tuh you." Many critics see this statement as the feminist declaration that Janie's story will inspire other women to demand self-fulfillment.

Janie Woods

See Janie Crawford

Tea Cake Woods

See Vergible Woods

Vergible Woods

When Tea Cake, a young man of twenty-five, enters Janie's life, he changes it forever. He does not possess the outward manifestations of power, namely wealth and position, that Jody did. Instead, he possesses an inner power that comes with self-knowledge and being comfortable with himself. When Janie marries Tea Cake, they move to

Jacksonville, and she is initiated into his world. At first he is afraid she will not want to be a part of his community. "You ain't usetuh folks lak dat," he tells her. But she assures him that she "aims tuh partake wid everything." When they move to the muck, then, to live amongst the migrant agricultural workers picking beans, Janie and Tea Cake's house becomes the center of the community, hosting dances and card games. Most importantly, Tea Cake allows Janie to feel like she belongs to this community in a way that Jody never let her belong to the Eatonville community. In fact, Tea Cake inspires two important developments in Janie's growth by encouraging her to accept herself and to feel at home in the black community. The space he creates for her that makes these two things possible is a loving relationship that satisfies Janie's spiritual needs, rather than focusing on the material wants that had defined her two previous marriages.

Their relationship is more equal as Tea Cake teaches her how to play checkers, hunt, and fish, activities from which Jody had excluded her because of her gender. Tea Cake almost becomes an idealized male figure in the book as he provides all of the support and love that has been lacking in Janie's life. However, he also falls back on attitudes of male dominance in his relationship with Janie. Many critics have seen his beating of Janie as an indication that Hurston believed all men possessed the need to overpower women and be the "boss." But Tea Cake is a part of Janie's life for only two years. As they try to escape the devastation of a hurricane in the Everglades, Tea Cake rescues Janie from a rabid dog, only to be bitten himself. By the time they discover Tea Cake's illness, it is too late. When he tries to kill Janie in his madness, she is forced to shoot him to protect herself.

Themes

Zora Neale Hurston's *Their Eyes Were Watching God* charts the development of an African American woman living in the 1920s and 1930s as she searches for her true identity.

Search for Self

Although the novel follows Janie through three relationships with men, most critics see its main theme to be Janie's search for herself. She must fight off the influences of her grandmother, who encourages her to sacrifice self-fulfillment for security, and her first two husbands, who stifle her development. Her second husband, Jody, has an especially negative impact on Janie's growth as his bourgeois aspirations turn her into a symbol of his stature in the town. She is not allowed to be her self, but must conform to his notions of propriety, which means she cannot enjoy the talk of the townsfolk on the porch, let alone participate in it. After he is elected mayor, she is asked to give "a few words uh encouragement," but Jody interrupts the applause by telling the town, "man wife don't know nothin' 'bout no speech-makin'. Ah never married her for her nothin' lak dat. She's uh woman and her place is in de home." After this, Janie feels "cold," realizing that by cutting her off, Jody has prevented her from deciding for herself whether or not she even wanted to give a speech. Throughout the rest of her marriage, Janie must bury her own desires to the point where she loses sight of them altogether. But after Jody's death she feels a freedom she has never known.

When the young Tea Cake enters her life, she decides that she has done what Jody and the town have wanted her to do long enough, so she rejects their ideas for her future and marries a younger man. Her relationship with Tea Cake allows her to find herself in a way that had not been possible before. But some critics see Tea Cake as another obstacle to Janie's development. In some ways, their relationship is conventional in the sense that Janie willingly defers to his judgment and follows him on his adventures. "Once upon uh time, Ah never 'spected nothin', Tea Cake, but being' dead from the standin' still and tryin' tuh laugh," she tells him. "But you come 'long and made somethin' out me." Statements like this have caused critics to question how successful Janie is at discovering her true self. Some see the ending as a reaffirmation that a woman must find herself on her own. By killing Tea Cake in self-defense, although she deeply regrets having to do so, Janie has come full circle in her development. She now knows who she is and has found "peace." In the closing lines the narrator tells us, "She pulled in her horizon like a great fish-net," indicating that she no longer has to seek for meaning outside of herself in the world; she has found it within herself.

Language and Meaning

Integral to Janie's search for self is her quest to become a speaking subject. Language is depicted in the novel as the means by which one becomes a full-fledged member of the community and, hence, a full human being. In Eatonville, the men engage in "eternal arguments, … a contest in hyperbole and carried on for no other reason." These contests in language are the central activities in the town, but only the men are allowed to participate. Janie especially regrets being excluded, but "gradually, she pressed her teeth together and learned to hush." But the dam of repressed language erupts when Jody ridicules her aging body in front of the men in the store. Her speech then becomes a weapon as she tells him (and everyone else), "When you pull down yo' britches, you look lak de change uh life." By comparing him to a woman going through menopause, she attacks his manhood in an irretrievable way. Janie has gained her voice, and in the process has metaphorically killed her husband, whose strength has resided in her silence and submission. Later, when Janie and Tea Cake are on the muck, Janie becomes a full member of the community, as signified by her ability as a speaking subject. "The men held big arguments here like they used to on the store porch. Only here, she could listen and laugh and even talk some herself if she wanted to. She got so she could tell big stories herself from listening to the rest." At the end of the book, Janie's return to tell her story to the town, through Pheoby, signals to some critics her reintegration in the community. Others, though, believe she is still excluded because she will not speak to them directly.

Topics for Further Study

- Research the conditions under which southern blacks lived during the Great Depression and compare to the plight of migrant workers on the muck in *Their Eyes Were Watching God.*
- Research the feminist movement from the early twentieth century to today. Based on your understanding of what a feminist was then and is now, argue whether Janie can or should be considered a feminist by contemporary scholars.
- Study the relationships between wealthy white patrons and the writers of the Harlem Renaissance

and argue whether *Their Eyes Were Watching God* is meant to appeal to white readers of the time or is directed only at black readers.

- Study the historic debates between Booker T. Washington and W. E. B. DuBois and, based on your reading of *Their Eyes Were Watching God*, create a response based on how you think Zora Neale Hurston would have responded to the fundamental issues of racial progress and race relations.

Race and Racism

Although there is very little discussion of relations between whites and blacks in the novel, racism and class differences are shown to have infected the African-American community. The supposed biological and cultural superiority of whiteness hovers over the lives of all the black characters in the book, as Janie witnesses the moral bankruptcy of those who value whiteness over their own black selves. Joe Starks is on his way to Eatonville when Janie meets him, because he is tired of being subservient to whites. He intends in an all-black town to have power over others, a kind of power that is modeled on that of white men. He possesses a "bow-down command in his face," and his large white house impresses the town because it makes the rest of the houses in town resemble "servants' quarters surrounding the 'big house,'" reflecting the housing arrangements of plantations during slavery. He also buys a desk like those owned by prominent white men in the neighboring town of Maitland and adopts behaviors which mimic the habits of middle-class whites. For Jody, success is measured by standards adopted from the white community, and as a result, he looks down on the townsfolk as "common" and even as his inferiors. One of the men comments, "You kin feel a switch in his hand when he's talking to yuh." Janie's rejection of Jody's feelings of superiority and his emphasis on attaining bourgeois respectability have led many critics to see the novel as a critique of middle-class blacks who had gained some prestige in the 1920s but had also lost their connection with the roots of the black community, the folk.

This critique becomes more explicit in Janie and Tea Cake's dismissal of Mrs. Turner's feelings of superiority over dark-skinned blacks. As a fairskinned and financially well-off mulatto, Mrs. Turner desires to separate herself and Janie, who is also mulatto, from the "black folks." She tells Janie, "We oughta lighten up de race," and "Us oughta class off." But Janie responds, "Us can't *do* it. We'se uh mingled people and all of us got black kinfolks as well as yaller kinfolks." For Janie, there are no divisions in the black community. She has moved easily from her high-class position in Eatonville to her life amongst the folk with Tea Cake, and together they have welcomed the black workers from the Bahamas, who had previously been ostracized from the African-Americans on the muck. In addition, Mrs. Turner's racist ideas are ridiculed by the narrator, who writes, "Behind her crude words was a belief that somehow she and others through worship could attain her paradise—a heaven of straight-haired, thin-lipped, high-nose boned white seraphs. The physical impossibilities in no way injured faith." Racism and division within the African-American community are finally revealed as not only ridiculous but as tragic, as a woman like Mrs. Turner is consumed by self hatred, the inherent by-product of her disdain of blackness. Only through a loving acceptance of all things black can one become a full, healthy human being, as Janie learns.

Style

Narration

Although the framing device of Janie telling Pheoby her story sets up the novel as Janie's story, it is not told in the first person. Instead, a narrative voice tells most of the story, and there has been much discussion of whose voice this is. Claire Crabtree, writing in *Southern Literary Journal*, argues that it is "always close to but not identical with Janie's consciousness," indicating that the omniscient narrator, who knows more about other characters' thoughts than Janie could know herself, is also closely aligned with the heroine. The narrator also uses free indirect speech at many points to convey Janie's thoughts, another indication that the narrator and Janie's consciousness are closely aligned. But Henry Louis Gates, Jr. in his *The Signifying Monkey*, argues that the narrative voice "echoes and aspires to the status of the impersonality, anonymity, and authority of the black vernacular tradition, a nameless, selfless tradition, at once collective and compelling." The narrator, then, who speaks in standard English, while the characters speak in black dialect, becomes, according to Gates, more and more representative of the black community as it progressively adopts the patterns of black vernacular speech. The narrative voice takes on the aspect of oral speech, telling not only Janie's story, but many other stories as well. For example, Nanny's voice takes over as she tells the story of Janie's heritage, and the voices on the porch also take over for long stretches as their "arguments" tell the story of life in Eatonville. In essence, there are many storytellers within the larger story of Janie's life, and many voices inform the novel.

Folklore

One of the most unique features of *Their Eyes Were Watching God* is its integration of folklore with fiction. Hurston borrows literary devices from the black rural oral tradition, which she studied as an anthropologist, to further cement her privileging of that tradition over the Western literary tradition. For example, she borrows the technique of repetition in threes found commonly in folklore in her depiction of Janie's three marriages. Also, in the words of Claire Crabtree, "Janie follows a pattern familiar to folklorists of a young person's journey from home to face adventure and various dangers, followed by a triumphant homecoming." In addition, Janie returns "richer and wiser" than she left, and she is ready to share her story with Pheoby, intending that the story be repeated, as a kind of folktale to be passed on.

Harlem Renaissance

The Harlem Renaissance, which experienced its heyday in Harlem in the 1920s but also flourished well into the 1930s, was an outpouring of creative innovation among blacks that celebrated the achievements of black intellectuals and artists. The initial goal of the writers of the Harlem Renaissance was to overcome racism and convince the white public that African-Americans were more intelligent than the stereotypes of docile, ignorant blacks that pervaded the popular arena. In order to do so, then, most of the early writers associated with the movement imitated the themes and styles of mainstream, white literature. But later writers felt that African-American literature should depict the unique and debilitating circumstances in which blacks lived, confronting their white audiences with scenes of brutal racism. Zora Neale Hurston, considered the most important female member of the Harlem Renaissance, felt that the writings of

African-Americans should celebrate the speech and traditions of black people. The use of dialect in *Their Eyes Were Watching God* caused much controversy among other black writers of the day when it was first published because many felt that such language in the mouths of black characters perpetuated negative stereotypes about blacks as ignorant, but critics today agree that the novel's celebration of black language was the most important contribution Hurston made to African-American literature.

Historical Context

The Great Depression

For southern farmers, both black and white, who did not enjoy the prosperity of northern industrial centers, the Great Depression had begun in the 1920s, well before the stock market crash of 1929. Factors such as soil erosion, the attack of the boll weevil on cotton crops, and the increasing competition from foreign markets led to widespread poverty amongst southern farmers. The majority of African Americans were still farming in the South and they were much harder hit than the white population, even after the advent of President Roosevelt's New Deal. The numbers of blacks on relief were three to four times higher than the number of whites, but relief organizations discriminated by race; some would not help blacks altogether, while others gave lower amounts of aid to blacks than they did to whites. Such practices led one NAACP leader to call the program "the same raw deal." Many critics have criticized *Their Eyes Were Watching God* for ignoring the plight of African-American farmers in the South during the 1920s and 30s, although Hurston does briefly describe the downtrodden migrant workers who come to pick beans on the muck. "Skillets, beds, patched up spare inner tubes all hanging and dangling from the ancient cars on the outside and hopeful humanity, herded and hovered on the inside, chugging on to the muck. People ugly from ignorance and broken from being poor."

The Great Migration and the Harlem Renaissance

A large number of African Americans fought in the First World War under the banner of freedom, only to return home to find how far they were from such a goal. By 1920, over one million blacks had fled the South, where they had little chance of rising out of poverty, and migrated to the industrial centers of the North where they obtained jobs in factories and packing houses, eventually making up as much as twenty percent of the industrial work force there. The migration of blacks to northern cities caused whites to fear that their jobs would be threatened, and increased racial tensions erupted in race riots in 1917. Nonetheless, many blacks began to vocally demand an end to discrimination. Out of this climate came calls for a "New Negro," who would be filled with racial pride and demand justice for his people. While earlier black leaders, represented by Booker T. Washington, had accepted segregation and preached cooperation and patience, new black leaders like W. E. B. DuBois insisted that concessions and appeasements were not the correct approach, and that complete equality could only be achieved by demanding it without compromise. DuBois also believed that the "Talented Tenth," his name for the small percentage of educated blacks, must lead the way for the masses of blacks who still lived in poverty and lacked educational opportunities. DuBois's ideas were reflected in the newly formed black middle class, which, although small, sought to exert an influence on behalf of all blacks. The new efforts of this black elite were centered in Harlem, where a large percentage of migrating blacks ended up, turning the area into a rich, thriving center of black culture. The new energy generated there by jazz musicians, writers, artists, actors, and intellectuals became known as the Harlem Renaissance. This artistic and intellectual movement confronted the racial prejudices of white America by demanding equal recognition for their talent and by depicting the injustices experienced by African-Americans. But ironically, although the artists of the Harlem Renaissance intended their works to promote better conditions for blacks less fortunate than themselves, few blacks around the country were even aware of the movement. In fact, it was more often whites who comprised the audiences and readerships of the products of the Harlem Renaissance. A cult of the primitive, which celebrated all things exotic and sensual, had become all the rage in New York and many wealthy whites flocked to Harlem to witness and participate in the revelry. But wealthy whites were essential to the livelihood of many black artists and writers who relied on their patronage, a fact regretted by many who felt that the artistic products of African Americans were muted to appeal to the tastes of the whites they depended on. Although the stock market crash of 1929 brought much of the activity in Harlem to an end, the creative energies of those involved had not abated, and many, like Zora Neale Hurston, produced their best work through the 1930s.

Compare & Contrast

- **1920s and '30s:** The numbers of unemployed African Americans during the Great Depression was as much as 25% in northern cities, and well over 50% in many southern cities, figures that were three to four times higher than the number of unemployed whites.
  Today: Unemployment among African-Americans averages between 10 and 11%, higher than the 4.5 to 5% among whites.
- **1920s and '30s:** Blues and jazz flourished from New Orleans to Harlem. Although these indigenous American music forms were the dominant mode of expression for the oppressed black culture, they also attracted a large audience of whites.
  Today: Rap and hip-hop are the major musical forms that express the unique experiences of black culture in America's ghettos, but they also have many non-black fans, not only in America, but all over the world.
- **1920s and '30s:** In the South, Jim

Crow laws dictated that blacks and whites use separate drinking fountains, eat in separate restaurants, and learn in separate schools. In the North, although such laws did not exist, blacks were more subtly excluded from better jobs, schools, and neighborhoods, creating black ghettos in the major cities.

Today: Affirmative action plans to end discrimination in hiring have been in place for fifteen years. Some people are now calling for their abolishment, claiming the goal has been achieved, while others believe there is still a long way to go.

- **1920s and '30s:** Although many women writers participated in the Harlem Renaissance, they experienced the prejudice of their male counterparts, who excluded all but a chosen few of them from the anthologies and prestigious periodicals.

  Today: African-American women writers are experiencing their own "Renaissance," as represented by Toni Morrison's receiving the Nobel Prize for Literature in 1993. Most contemporary critics agree that some of the most important literature being produced today is by African-American women, many of whom claim a direct heritage from Zora Neale Hurston.

Race Colonies

After the Civil War, former slaves formed a number of all-black towns all over the South, in an effort to escape the segregation and discrimination they experienced amongst whites. By 1914, approximately thirty such towns were in existence. Eatonville, Florida, the town where Zora Neale Hurston grew up and the setting for much of *Their Eyes Were Watching God*, was the first such town to be incorporated and to win the right of self-governance. In Eatonville, the Jim Crow laws, that segregated public schools, housing, restaurants, theaters, and drinking fountains all over the South, did not exist.

Critical Overview

When *Their Eyes Were Watching God* first appeared, it was warmly received by white critics. Lucille Tompkins of the *New York Times Book Review* called it "a well nigh perfect story—a little sententious at the start, but the rest is simple and beautiful and shining with humor." But many of Hurston's fellow writers of the Harlem Renaissance criticized the novel for not addressing "serious" issues, namely strained race relations. Alain Locke, reviewing for *Opportunity*, recognized the author's "gift for poetic phrase, for rare dialect, and folk humor," but he asks, "when will the Negro novelist of maturity ... come to grips with motive fiction and social document fiction?" Richard Wright, in his review in *New Masses*, had even more scathing objections to the novel. According to Wright, "Miss Hurston *voluntarily* continues in her novel the tra dition which was *forced* upon the Negro in the theater, that is, the minstrel technique that makes the 'white folks' laugh." Wright felt that instead of taking on "serious" subjects, she writes to entertain "a white audience whose chauvinistic tastes she knows how to satisfy." Many objected to the use of dialect in the novel, a difficult subject for Harlem Renaissance writers who felt that black speech had been exploited and ridiculed by mainstream theater and literature. As a result, many were reluctant to try to realistically depict the speech patterns of the black folk, and they saw in Hurston's use of dialect a degrading picture of rural blacks.

As a result of such criticisms, *Their Eyes Were Watching God* soon disappeared from print. But in the late 1960s, when interest in African-American and women's studies began to take hold, a number of African-American women across the country rediscovered the book and made it an underground sensation. Photocopies of the novel circulated at conferences, and Alice Walker's essay "Looking for Zora," published in *Ms.* magazine in 1975, galvanized efforts to get the novel back into print. Since 1978, it has been widely available, and the scholarly interest in it has been intense. In fact, previous judgements against the novel have been overturned by a number of respectable critics who have helped establish *Their Eyes Were Watching God* as a classic of African-American literature and helped procure it a prominent position in the American literary canon.

Most significantly, recent critics have recognized a celebration of black culture in the novel that belies any notion that Hurston is pandering to a white audience. As Cheryl Wall explains, in her article "Zora Neale Hurston: Changing Her Own Words," She asserted that black people, while living in a racist society that denied their humanity, had created an "alternative culture that validated their worth as human beings." And, she argues, by invoking this culture, Hurston shows us that black men and women "attained personal identity not by transcending the culture but by embracing it." One way that Hurston embraced the culture of rural, southern blacks, was to depict its folklore and language in a way that relished its creativity. Contemporary critics praise her for this above all else, for in her search for a suitable language for African-American literature, she initiated an effort to free black language from domination by the white culture. Henry Louis Gates, Jr., explains the significance of this act: "For Hurston, the search for a telling form of language, indeed the search for a black literary language itself, defines the search for the self." In this way, critics have been able to show that Hurston, far from ignoring the serious social issues of her day, was engaged in a serious project of resuscitating a language and culture that was in danger of being corrupted by racist oppression. In fact, Gay Wilentz argues, in *Faith of a (Woman) Writer*, that the novel is one of "resistance" because it portrays "the pressure of the dominant culture on the thoughts and actions of the all-black community of Eatonville as well as blacks as a whole." In other words, although she largely ignored the overt racism that critics of the Harlem Renaissance wanted her to address, she explored the more subtle and perhaps more dangerous kind of racism that infects the black culture and makes it despise itself. The racial pride that Hurston preached, then, was as radical a statement as any of the Harlem Renaissance, contemporary critics argue.

Although scholars have been eager to embrace the novel's celebration of black culture, much more problematic has been understanding and accepting its perspective on gender. With the book's rediscovery in the 1960s, feminists lauded it as an expression of female self-development and empowerment. More recently, though, many scholars have begun to question such a reading. Jennifer Jordon argues, for example, in her article in *Tulsa Studies in Women's Literature*, that "Janie's struggle for identity and self-direction remains stymied. She never defines herself outside the scope of her marital or romantic involvements." Furthermore, as Mary Helen Washington insists in her article "'I Love the Way Janie Crawford Left Her Husbands': Emergent Female Hero," Janie never becomes a speaking subject, because "Hurston's strategy of having much of Janie's tale told by an omniscient third person rather than by a first person narrator undercuts the development of Janie's 'voice.' " But most troubling to critics has been the fact that Janie seems to discover herself in the context of a relationship with a man, Tea Cake, rather than on her own, a defect that many see as remedied by Janie's killing of Tea Cake. "[A]s a feminist," Claire Crabtree argues, Hurston "did not want Janie to find fulfillment in a man, but rather in her new-found self." But for others, the book does not end there, rather with her return to Eatonville, which seems to signal an end to her self-exploration, according to Washington, who claims that "left without a man, she (Janie) exists in a position of stasis." But Wall refuses to read the ending as "tragic." "For with Tea Cake as her guide, Jan[i]e has explored the soul of her culture and learned how to value herself."

Sources

Claire Crabtree, "The Confluence of Folklore, Feminism and Black Self-Determination in Zora Neale Hurston's *Their Eyes Were Watching God,*" *Southern Literary Journal*, Vol. 17, no. 2, Spring, 1985, pp. 54-66.

Henry Louis Gates, Jr., *The Signifying Monkey*, Oxford, 1988.

Jennifer Jordon, "Feminist Fantasies: Zora Neale Hurston's *Their Eyes Were Watching God,*" *Tulsa Studies in Women's Literature*, Vol. 7, Spring, 1988, pp. 105-17.

Alain Locke, review in *Opportunity*, June 1, 1938, reprinted in *Zora Neale Hurston: Critical Perspectives Past and Present*, edited by Henry Louis Gates, Jr. and K. A. Appiah, Amistad, 1993, p. 18.

Lucille Tompkins, review in *New York Times Book Review*, September 26, 1937, reprinted in *Zora Neale Hurston: Critical Perspectives Past and Present*, edited by Henry Louis Gates, Jr. and K. A. Appiah, Amistad, 1993, pp. 18-19.

Alice Walker, "Looking for Zora," in *In Search of Our Mothers' Gardens*, Harcourt Brace Jovanovich, 1983, pp. 93-116.

Cheryl Wall, "Zora Neale Hurston: Changing Her Own Words," in *Zora Neale Hurston: Critical Perspectives Past and Present*, edited by Henry

Louis Gates, Jr. and K. A. Appiah, Amistad, 1993, pp. 78-97.

Mary Helen Washington, "'I Love the Way Janie Crawford Left Her Husbands': Emergent Female Hero," in *Zora Neale Hurston: Critical Perspectives Past and Present*, edited by Henry Louis Gates, Jr. and K. A. Appiah, Amistad, 1993, pp. 98-109.

Gay Wilentz, "Defeating the False God: Janie's Self-Determination in Zora Neale Hurston's *Their Eyes Were Watching God,"* in *Faith of a (Woman) Writer*, edited by Alice Kessler-Harris and William McBrien, Greenwood Press, 1988, pp. 285-91.

Richard Wright, review in *New Masses*, October 5, 1937, reprinted in *Zora Neale Hurston: Critical Perspectives Past and Present*, edited by Henry Louis Gates, Jr. and K. A. Appiah, Amistad, 1993, pp. 16-17.

For Further Study

Sharon Davie, "Free Mules, Talking Buzzards, and Cracked Plates: The Politics of Dislocation in *Their Eyes Were Watching God"* in *PMLA*, May, 1993, pp. 446-459.

> Scholarly article which examines the relationships among control, reason, and language in the novel.

Robert E. Hemenway, *Zora Neale Hurston*, Illinois, 1977.

> A popular biography of the writer which includes a good discussion of her work and its relationship to her life.

Karla F. C. Holloway, *Moorings & Metaphors: Figures of Culture and Gender in Black Women's Literature*, Rutgers, 1992.

> A book-length study which considers the work of several black women writers and several of Hurston's works in addition to *Their Eyes Were Watching God.*

Pearlie Peters, "Women and Assertive Voice in Hurston's Fiction and Folklore," in *The Literary Griot*, Spring/Fall, 1992, pp. 100-10.

> An article which discusses the African-American oral tradition and

its social significance.

Priscilla Wald, "Becoming 'Colored': The Self-Authorized Language of Difference in Zora Neale Hurston," in *American Literary History*, Spring, 1990, pp. 79-100.

Scholarly article which discusses Hurston's ability to be both the observer and the observed and which compares her fiction to her studies of folklore.

Alice Walker, "Zora Neale Hurston: A Cautionary Tale and a Partisan View," in *In Search of Our Mothers' Gardens*, Harcourt Brace Jovanovich, 1983, pp. 83-92.

An essay which discusses Walker's discovery of Hurston's work.

CPSIA information can be obtained
at www.ICGtesting.com
Printed in the USA
BVHW050742250821
615017BV00010B/1590

9 781375 399029